HOUSTON PUBL

Conversations with Primo Levi

Other works by the same author,
translated into English,
and published by The Marlboro Press:

MEMORIAL
THE FIFTH ESTATE
LIFE EVERLASTING
THE STORY OF SIRIO

Ferdinando Camon

Conversations with Primo Levi

Translated by John Shepley

The Marlboro Press
Marlboro, Vermont

R0126144490
numca

HOUSTON PUBLIC LIBRARY

First English language edition.

Translation copyright © 1989 by John Shepley. All rights reserved. No part of this book may be reproduced in any form without permission in writing from the publisher, except by a reviewer who may quote brief passages in a review to be printed in a magazine or newspaper.

Originally published in Italian under the title
AUTORITRATTO DI PRIMO LEVI
Copyright © 1987 Edizioni Nord-Est, Padova

The publication of the present volume has been made possible by a grant from the National Endowment for the Arts.

Manufactured in the United States of America

Library of Congress Catalog Card Number 88-64143

ISBN 0-910395-48-9

Contents

This long critical conversation with Primo Levi took place over several meetings, and was thoroughly checked by him in 1986, one Sunday in May. It began with the intention (on my side) of drawing up a portrait of Primo Levi and (on his) a self-portrait, and was meant to be included in a new, often-planned edition of my book of interviews entitled *Il mestiere di scrittore*. That project has now been shelved. Since I have often been asked (by Italian newspapers, the weekly magazine *Panorama*, the French daily *Libération*) for portions of this interview, and it has accordingly only appeared in bits and pieces, it seems to me both right and proper to offer it in its entirety, so that each part, each statement, can be seen in its true context, as it relates to other statements and to the whole body of discourse. Which, incidentally, is what Levi himself wanted.

The method we followed in arranging this conversation was quite simple. To begin with, I prepared a systematic set of questions, issues, and problems, making sure that they were related to the entire life and work of Primo Levi. This was to be the "outline" that would guide and mark the stages of the whole dialogue, as I anticipated it. It was the same set of "questions" that I would have had to deal with had I been writing a critical study of Primo Levi. He would be able to go over it and combine it in any way he liked with those questions that would have been unavoidable for him had he been writing a critical self-portrait. That indeed is exactly what happened, and he made a considerable number of additions and combinations. Our agreement, in any case, was that in our talks we would use these suggestions merely as guidelines, with the freedom to strike out in any direction in which the dialogue might take a turn. Having agreed to this, we were to see each other several times. The final text of the interview would be checked by him, on the typescript, and he would be completely at liberty to make any changes or corrections.

And so it happened: the final draft of the dialogue bears a significant number of changes, in Primo Levi's handwriting, and all of them without exception have been observed.

Primo Levi was a marvelous conversationalist: precise, meticulous, and with frequent and pertinent mental associations. The first of our meetings, the one that set up the structure and much of the development of this conversation, took place in 1982. The last one, as I said, was in 1986, a Sunday in late May. That is to say, a few months, not even a year, before his death. All our meetings took place in Turin. The first in the Palace Hotel, in front of the railroad station. The last, in his home. The others in local restaurants.

Levi had a healthy respect for the peace and quiet of his own home, and had therefore wanted to meet me somewhere outside for the first interview, which was expected to be long and tiring. I waited for him in the street, in front of the hotel. Terrorism was still rampant. I remember it because of the scene in my memory: in the square in front of the hotel some twenty youths—short, husky, dark-haired and swarthy, dressed in leather jackets and boots—were yelling raucously, shoving each other and laughing. By the time Levi arrived, they were all lined up with their faces to the wall and their hands in the air. A number of plainclothesmen were calmly searching them, while other police, their guns ready, stood guard a few yards away. With armed clashes, arrests, jailings, and official investigations, terrorism was on the wane, but Turin had been one of its strongholds.

FERDINANDO CAMON

Levi arrived, short, pale, courteous. He suggested we go immediately to a corner of the
hotel lobby and begin the interview.

His hair and beard were white, the beard
whiter than the hair. His look was almost ironic,
his smile almost playful. A very orderly mind,
with detailed, precise memories. At a certain
point he picked up the sheet of paper with the
questions and on the back drew the layout of
Auschwitz: with the central concentration
camp, the outlying ones, and the number of
prisoners. He spoke in a low voice, without
getting excited, with no outbursts—that is to
say, without rancor.

I have often wondered about the reason for
this mildness, this gentleness. The only answer
that comes to mind, even today, is the following:
Levi did not shout, did not assail, did not accuse,
because he didn't *want* to shout. He wanted
something much more: to *make* people shout.
He renounced his own reaction in exchange for
the reaction of the rest of us. He took a long-
range view. His mildness, his gentleness, his
smile—which had something shy, almost child-
like about it—were actually his weapons.

FERDINANDO CAMON

4

1. The devil in history

Camon: The same year you were born (1919) the National Socialist Party was founded in Germany and in Italy Mussolini founded the *fasci di combattimento*. It almost seems that your life was marked from the very beginning. When you were a child, did they talk about these things in your home? Was there a time of premonition, of foreboding?

Levi: Not really. My family was a bourgeois one. In the years I was born no one—in Italy at least—spoke of ostracizing the Jews. My father, who had worked for a long time in Hungary and France, had had certain experiences and knew what anti-Semitism meant there. He had witnessed Béla Kun's revolution in Budapest, and had a traumatic memory of it, but he told me very little about it, extraordinarily little. As a bourgeois, he had been frightened by Béla Kun's attempt, even doubly frightened, because Béla Kun was a Jew and known as such in Hungary. All the same in '19 he had enacted a soviet constitution. My father was afraid of Communism, and afraid of the reaction to Communism, and afraid of the reaction to a Communist Jew.

As for the founding of the *fasci di combattimento* in Italy, all in all he didn't have much to say about it. I was born and grew up in a Fascist climate, even though my father wasn't a Fascist. He was opposed to Fascism for superficial reasons, he didn't care for the mummery, the parades, the lack of seriousness . . .

Camon: Matters of taste?

Levi: Mostly matters of taste. But I talked very little about it with my father, there was too much difference in age between the two of us, and there wasn't much communication. I think the fear he had felt in Hungary was still alive in him; it had been a bloody revolution. Later Béla Kun himself was killed, on Stalin's orders.

So, as for premonitions and forebodings in our house, I'd have to say no, there weren't any. I was too young, and my father had a tendency to be critical of everything. He died in '42—

fortunately for him, and for us, since he wouldn't have survived what happened later.

Camon: Then if there was a premonition, it was only a matter of months?

Levi: A few months. It wasn't even a premonition—by then it was all there.

Camon: You were twenty-three when Hitler decided on the so-called Final Solution in Germany. A year later you'd joined the partisans in the Valle d'Aosta, had been taken prisoner, and ended up in a concentration camp. Still you ended up there as a Jew, not as a partisan. If I remember correctly, here there was a choice on your part, I mean it was you who got them to recognize you as one rather than the other. I mention this detail because I think it would be interesting if we could make a comparison between the two "sins": the "sin" of being a Jew and the "sin" of being a partisan. Which was more dangerous?

Levi: Yes, I was the one who let them recognize me as a Jew. We seldom make decisions out of pure logic, and seldom for a single motive. I'd been caught with forged documents, all too obviously forged: among other things, I was supposed to have been born in Battipaglia, and the militiaman who caught (and hit) me was from Battipaglia, and right away this put me in a difficult position. I was suspected of being a Jew, there were rumors in the Valle d'Aosta that I was a Jew. The militiamen who captured me had told me, "If you're a partisan, we'll put you up against the wall; if you're a Jew, we'll send you to Carpi."

Camon: So your choice was determined by their threats.

Levi: Yes, but besides that the element of fatigue came into it, because they kept asking, and telling me, "We'll send you to a concentration camp and you'll stay there till the war's over in Italy; we don't hand anyone over to the Germans." And at the end there was also an element of pride: I would have been sorry if it hadn't come out that I, a very inept partisan (I hadn't done any military service, I didn't know the first thing about guns; I had one but I didn't know how to use it: I only fired one shot, because otherwise it was a waste of bullets) but a partisan all the same, was a Jew—to show that even the Jews can make up their minds to fight back.

Camon: Then you did have a weapon.

Levi: It was a small pistol, all inlaid with mother-of-pearl, I don't even know where it came from. A revolver with a tiny little cylinder, and a range of five meters. I can't remember now who'd given it to me. Anyway the partisan band we'd organized was one of the first, and we got caught, I think, in the first round-up that took place in all of Italy. So I was completely disarmed, morally as well: "armed defense" wasn't part of my world. There were many like me. Only the ones who later got used to it became fairly good partisans.

Camon: But when the militiamen said to you, "If you're Jews, we'll send you to a concentration camp for the rest of the war," were they lying?

Levi: I'm sure they were in good faith.

Camon: So things got bad later, let's say, when the people in charge of the situation changed?

Levi: I'm sure of it. And it happened when we were already at Carpi-Fossoli. We were being held by the Fascists, who didn't treat us badly. They let us write letters, let us receive packages, and swore to us on their "Fascist faith" that they'd keep us there till the end of the war.

Camon: Then you were handed over to the Germans. And here that question comes up which I don't think has been clearly answered, not even in books of first-hand testimony: why did the Germans feel such an acute aversion to the Jews? Here it's not something political, it's not something economic. There's something here that goes much deeper.

Levi: Ah, that's a terrible question, and I can only give a partial answer. In the first place, I must answer with an objection, because it's not correct to say that "the Germans" felt this hatred, which is a racial one. They felt it after some years of the Nazi regime. So the question leads to another one: why did the Germans accept Hitler? I've read a lot of books, even by famous historians, and I find they've all thrown up their hands at this problem, the problem of the consensus, the mass consensus, in Germany. I must say the same. All you can say of those who rejected Hitler is that they didn't accept him enthusiastically. Now, accepting Hitler also meant accepting his program of anti-Semitism. That's the problem.

Camon: In fact, they didn't have a strong resistance, not even later, when Nazism was in full swing. I mean a resistance in the Italian sense of the word.

Levi: No, no, they didn't. There were various patches of resistance—the White Rose, on the one hand; that right-wing officers' plot, on the other; what was left of the Communist Party; a few nuclei of resistance in the concentration camps on the part of German political prisoners—but they didn't get along with each other very well, and they even had trouble communicating. Probably also there was no resistance in our sense because it was a model police state. I don't know if you've read that excellent book by Hans Fallada, *Each Man Dies Alone*.[1] Anyone reading it can understand what Germany was like at that time. Fallada was an anti-Nazi and had already written *Little Man, What Now?*[2] But maybe we're getting a little too much off the point.

Camon: No, we're right at the crux of the matter. It's not a question of explaining one aspect of German behavior at the time of the Nazis, but all of that behavior, in general. And not just one moment in the history of the Germans, but a long governing principle, running through their mythology, their conversion—Freud called them "poorly baptized"—, their Lutheranism, their sense of salvation and perdition.

Levi: If you don't mind, I disagree with that interpretation. The Germans in Goethe's time weren't like that. Germany began to deviate in this direction later on. If you read Maupassant's stories about the Prussian occupation of France, you can see it was harsh, but not much different from that of other armies. And the Germans of the First World War were those of Remarque, they were no different from the French. Their war has been distorted by French and Italian propaganda, but the German trenches were no different from the Italian and French ones.

---

1. *Jeder stirbt für sich allein*. [1947].
2. *Kleiner Mann—was nunn?* [1932].

11

Camon: All the same, whenever their moral and religious movements start up again in a big way, they always draw on a reservoir of perdition, of damnation, of . . .

Levi: Of the demonic?

Camon: Of the demonic, which drags in and cancels out divinity itself . . .

Levi: Yes, the devil is a fundamental presence in their upbringing.

Camon: . . . with the result that there's not a glimmer of good, and the search for their own salvation can't avoid a hatred directed at God, which you can even see in Luther. They asked Luther, "How can one love this God?" and he replied, "Love him? On the contrary, I hate him." I mentioned Freud, calling the Germans "poorly baptized," precisely to indicate their continuous resistance to forms of homologation in European Christian civilization. From the times of the barbarian invasions to the Second World War, their irruptions into history have been no different from the irruption of the plague and the great epidemics. I'm reminded of that cardinal who called Hitler a "motorized Attila."

Levi: I should be the one to say these things.

Camon: It should be you, and in my opinion you do say them. You say them through my lips. The kind of pedagogical task that you perform with your narrative, that you perform for example in *Survival in Auschwitz*, consists in leading the reader by the hand to experience a certain reaction and pronounce a certain condemnation—without saying it yourself. For your part, you use the technique of suspending not only condemnation but judgment as well.

Levi: It's true that I refrained from formulating judgments in *Survival in Auschwitz*. I did so deliberately, because it seemed to me inopportune, not to say importunate, on the part of the witness, namely myself, to take the place of the judge. So I suspended any explicit judgment, while the implicit judgments are clearly there.

But I sincerely don't think I share this drastic judgment of yours about the Germans, which goes all the way back to the Teutons. Any overall judgment on the intrinsic, innate qualities of a people to me smells of racism. I mean to be immune to it, even if sometimes I have to make an effort. Actually I'm very interested in German culture, I've been studying—for some years now—the German language, and I have German friends. I absolutely don't feel the equivalent of the anti-Jewish aversion expressed by Hitler's Germans. It hasn't produced any conditioned reflexes in me. On the contrary, I'd say that the lasting curiosity I feel about the Germany of then and now excludes hatred.

Camon: I'm surprised, however, to a certain degree by this need to be neutral, to suspend judgment. For if the German says, "There's something murky in the Jew," and the Jew answers, "There's something murky in the German who talks like that," in the first case we can speak of anti-Semitism, but in the second we can't speak of anti-Germanism, because the Jew who said it would simply be speaking the truth.

Levi: I should be the one to say these things. It's odd that here I'm defending the Germans, and yet it's up to me to do so. I don't think that even in Hitler's Germany was anti-Semitism widespread at first. The German Jews were integrated, they were a bourgeoisie broadly assimilated into the German nation. This is something we know from many sources, and I even heard it from my father. In Germany the Jews were not so much the "other," not so alien as in Poland or Russia, as to produce offensive and defensive reflexes against whatever was different, or not-like-me. In my opinion, the weight of Hitler's personality was the determining factor in everything, even in this. I don't much believe in Tolstoy's thesis of history emerging from below, from a tide on which the Napoleons bob like corks. Because experience has shown me: I had a distinct impression in witnessing the rise of Nazism in Germany, and experiencing it firsthand, and then reading about it later, the impression of a curse, of something demonic—you spoke of it a moment ago, of the devil as a constant in German culture—being embodied in Hitler. And here I'm reminded again of Fallada, whom I mentioned a while back.

Fallada's *Each Man Dies Alone* seems to me important for this very reason. Fallada got his hands on some Gestapo files and found a true story on which he based a novel, about an old worker, an old German carpenter, an *Arbeitstier* or "workhorse," a passive, indifferent man, whose only concern was to do a good job as a carpenter.

He loses a son in the war. And then he comes in contact with the parents of other casualties. Very naively, he and his wife invent a method of resisting. Every Saturday they write a postcard, with very open, very naive anti-Nazi slogans on it: "This war will lead us to ruin," things like that. And they take a little stroll away from their home and stick it in the mailbox of some private house. This goes on for a year. I seem to remember they distribute something like 150,200 postcards. All these cards end up in the hands of the Gestapo, each within a few hours. The Gestapo official assigned to the case has only to mark the points where these cards have been left to see a circle of little flags emerge on the map of Berlin, because the husband and wife, so as not to get caught, each time took a fifteen-minute stroll away from their house, and each time in a different direction. So obviously the person responsible had to be at the center.

What seems to me a very important proof of the power of the police during the Hitler regime is that these postcards scorched the hand of every German who received one; they're afraid it's a provocation and immediately take it to the nearest police station. This shows how difficult it was to organize a resistance. There was only the will of Hitler, there was no opposition.

Camon: That's a "heroic" conception of history: history is made by the few, the rulers, the heroes whose will shakes the world like a wind, and all the people can do is cower.

Levi: Yes, I'm well aware that many don't share this conception, but it seems to me that, at least in cases like this, one must realize that the personal power of people like Hitler and Stalin— and not like Mussolini—have weighed heavily. For there's a qualitative leap between Germany before Hitler and Hitler's Germany. If you've seen films at the cinema or on TV of Hitler's speeches to the crowd, you've witnessed a tremendous spectacle. A mutual induction was formed, as between a cloud charged with electricity and the earth. It was an exchange of

16

lightning bolts. Hitler responded to the reaction that he himself provoked. And he gloried in it. I think—if such an observation makes sense— that had another man been in his place, things would have gone differently. Not even his henchmen could have taken his place, not even someone like Goering or Himmler. Maybe Goebbels, if he'd been picked.

Camon: So, you see history as a huge neurosis, transmitted by osmosis to the crowd?

Levi: At least in this case. I'm not a historian, I can't say if other times it happened differently. I've often thought (and hoped) that Hitler's Germany was unique, destined not to be repeated— the improbable fruit of the combination of various elements (and one of them was the personality of Hitler) which taken singly would not have led to serious consequences. It seems to me that today, on the Italian scene for example, this isn't happening, there's no hero, either good or bad, there's no protagonist. Maybe not even in Germany. Maybe that period that marked us, in the early part of the century, was destined to end, but it was a period of strong personalities. I'd also include Churchill.

Camon: You mean heroes who made everyone's will a continuation of their own will.

Levi: Yes, I'd really say so.

2. *The sin of being born*

Camon: So you spent a year in the concentration camp. The concentration camp, the metaphor par excellence for man's inhumanity to man, one of the major sins of history. Benjamin, however, said somewhere that the concentration camp is not an abnormal condition beyond comparison with the rest of the world. The concentration camp is nothing but the condensation of a condition common in the world. In short, the concentration camp itself mirrors the structures of every society: it too has its saved and its drowned, its oppressors and oppressed.

Levi: I have two things to say about that. The first with repugnance: this comparison of the world with the concentration camp arouses revulsion in us, those of us who have been "marked," "tattooed." No, that's not the way it is, it's not true that the Fiat factory is a concentration camp, or that the psychiatric hospital is a concentration camp. There's no gas chamber at Fiat. You can be very badly off in the psychiatric hospital, but there's no oven, there's an exit, and your family can come to visit. Those graffiti you sometimes see on walls, "Factory = concentration camp," "School = concentration camp," disgust me: it's not true. Nevertheless, and this is the second thing I have to say, they can be valid as metaphor. I said so myself in *Survival in Auschwitz*, that the concentration camp is a mirror of the external situation, but a distorting mirror. For example, the automatic and inevitable establishment of a hierarchy among the victims is a fact that has not been sufficiently discussed, the fact that the prisoner who gets ahead on the backs of his comrades exists everywhere.

Camon: Is it or isn't it a necessary condition for the functioning of the camp?

Levi: It's useful for the functioning of the camp. It was exploited by the Nazis, but even if it hadn't been encouraged, it existed anyway. Particularly where law turns out to be lacking, the law of the jungle is established, Darwinian law, by which the fittest, who are mostly the worst, prevail and survive by eating the living flesh of the others. It was a conspicuous phenomenon in the camps.

Here I have to digress for a moment. I lived through the concentration camp under the worst conditions, meaning as a Jew. Many diaries of political prisoners have very different stories to tell, but there's no contradiction. The conditions under which the political prisoners lived in the camps were different from ours, because they had a moral as well as political armor that most of us lacked. Some Jews, of course, were also political prisoners. I myself was to a certain extent, because I'd been a partisan: I did have a certain sense of reserve and of the duty to resist being sucked down into the depths. But my companions in the camp weren't politicals, they were the flotsam and jetsam, poor unfortunates who had five years of continuous persecution behind them, people who had escaped perhaps from Nazi Germany to Poland or Czechoslovakia, and then been overtaken by the Nazi tide, they'd escaped to Paris, to be overtaken there too and end up finally at Auschwitz; or else poor devils from the Ukraine, Byelorussia, or eastern Poland, with no contact with Western civilization, suddenly hurled into a situation they didn't understand. This was the human material I had around me. Among these unfortunates, there was no solidarity, none at all, and this lack was the first and biggest trauma. I and the others who'd been transported with me had thought, naively, "However bad it may be, we'll find comrades." It didn't turn out that way. We found enemies, not comrades.

Camon: I think that Christians and Catholics, people born and raised in a Christian and Catholic society, find themselves faced here with a problem they can't quite grasp, can't experience even in their imaginations, and therefore can't understand. I mean the problem of finding oneself having to pay for the sin of being born. Because I think this was the "sin" that distinguished the Jew from the political prisoner or the partisan or the POW. They were paying for a lost battle, or a political opposition, but the Jew for the mere fact of having been born had this "sin" to pay for: the sin of existing. He was supposed to disappear. The sin of being born is a concept that had been worked out in certain currents of Greek philosophy, and later in certain tendencies of non-theistic existentialism. But in its essence it remains a concept that can't really be experienced by Christians.

Levi: This condemnation was indeed experienced as an incomprehensible injustice. Each of us came with explanations valid for himself alone. My own perception was that it had to do with madness, a methodical madness.

Camon: And the awareness that you were all suffering a common injustice didn't unite you?

Levi: Not enough. For many reasons. The fundamental reason was the lack of communication, and this was the second trauma. Few of us Italian Jews understood German or Polish—very few. I knew a few words of German. Under those conditions, the language barrier was fatal. Almost all the Italians died from it. Because from the very first days they didn't understand the orders, and this wasn't allowed, wasn't tolerated. They didn't understand the orders and couldn't say so, they couldn't make themselves understood. They heard a shout, because Germans, German soldiers, always shout . . .

Camon: To "give vent to a centuries-old rage."

Levi: That's what I wrote in *Survival in Auschwitz*. And this was the third trauma. For them it's natural, it goes on in their army even now: orders get shouted. Well, the order got shouted but wasn't understood, and therefore the Italians always got there last. You'd ask for information, news, explanations from your bunk mate, and he didn't listen and didn't understand.

This fact was already the first big obstacle to unity, to recognizing ourselves as comrades.

I—I've always said I was lucky—I found I had a little bit of the German language at my command, as a chemist I'd studied it, and so I was able to establish some sort of communication with the non-Italians, and this was essential for understanding where I was living, the rules of

23

the place. And also for perceiving that sense of unity you speak of. In fact, I remember that when contacts were established with some friendly French, Hungarian, and Greek prisoners, we felt that we'd taken a step upward.

Camon: Those conditions, of course, formed a substantial part of the concentration camp—they formed the camp. The camp was conceived in such a way that people couldn't survive. And this brings us back to that problem we touched on before, of how it was possible for a collective culture and way of life—I don't say everybody's, but anyway collective—to arrive at the point of deciding that it had to make a whole race expiate the sin of existing. You spoke before of the projection of the will and morality of a leader. I have a feeling that there must have been much more, that such a culture must already have had within itself the germs of a conception of existence as sin.

Levi: It doesn't seem to me that you can load onto a German collectivity (even a limited one) the wish to "punish" the Jews by exterminating them. Everyone in Germany knew of the existence of the concentration camps. A few people had come out of the specifically political ones, like Mauthausen and Buchenwald, and were able to tell about it. Besides, the news of the existence of the camps was useful to the Nazis, and was an effective deterrent. On the other hand, the program for exterminating the Jews and gypsies was kept as secret as possible—it was too horrible a piece of news to meet with approval even in National Socialist party circles. And nobody got out of the concentration camps set up for pure and total massacre: Treblinka, Chelmno, Maidenek, and a few others (Auschwitz is in a class by itself, we'll speak of it later). It's certainly not by chance that they were all located outside the German borders: the Germans weren't supposed to know what was going on in them. For the same reason the extermination of German mental patients had to be kept secret, but since this happened of necessity in Germany, something leaked out, a few courageous clergymen protested, and the program was halted.

For these reasons I find it impossible to impute this "death wish" to the German people, or even to a substantial portion of them. One can and should, however, accuse the German people of cowardice: the Germans could have known much more about the extermination if they'd wanted to, and if the few who knew had had the courage to speak, but this didn't happen. Those who knew kept silent, those who didn't know were afraid to ask questions—eyes, ears, and mouths stayed shut. It's certainly true that state terrorism is a very strong weapon, one that it's very hard to resist, but it's also true that the German people, on the whole, didn't even try to resist.

I've had some hair-raising exchanges of letters with Germans. I can tell you one case that I heard about by letter.

Camon: As a result of your book being published in Germany?

Levi: No, by chance. I'd been corresponding—I still am—with a German lady who knew some of the chemists who worked where I was working, but on the other side. I told about one of them in *The Periodic Table*, in the chapter "Vanadium." But I heard about another case from this lady, the case of H., an official, a chemist, my age, my double, an organic chemist like me. This man worked in a rubber factory at Ludwigshafen, and was offered a job at Auschwitz. He didn't really know what it was, but the Ludwigshafen factory where he worked often got bombed, because it was within the range of the American bombers. Ludwigshafen was, and is, an important German manufacturing center. The Germans had duplicated the Ludwigshafen factory at Auschwitz, the Auschwitz factory (Buna) was identical—they'd used the same plans all over again there. Because there there was coal, there was water, there was slave labor, and it was out of range of the bombers. H. thinks it over, he is engaged to be married, he goes to take a look, finds the factory under construction, and agrees to be transferred there. He goes back, takes his wife (or future wife, I don't know which) and the furniture, settles down at Auschwitz, works there for six or eight months, and then it's all over. He goes back where he came from, and his friends, who are decent people, ask him, "Where've you been?" And he doesn't speak. Neither during his time off while he was working there, nor afterwards, did he ever speak. He'd get drunk, he'd play the piano and drink. They used to ask him, "What did you see?" and he'd answer, "Oh, there's a concentration camp nearby." That was all. I was planning to interview this Herr H., but in the meantime he died. There's his wife, but I can't bring myself to go and bother her.

This to me seems to typify the behavior of the Germans, who didn't speak and didn't hear so as not to become guilty of this thing they sensed.

Camon: So it's repression?

Levi: No, I wouldn't call it repression, because repression is internal. You repress something you know. Here instead the shutters get closed before it's known.

Camon: So, in your opinion, that man in the concentration camp hadn't known, he'd refused to see, to become aware?

Levi: Yes, he didn't want to know, he didn't want to have to speak.

"bone crushers," to crush, grind, torture, destroy the leaders, and make them disappear, first of all the Communist leaders, secondly the Social Democrats, Catholics, Protestants, and some Jews—in short, those who were thorns in the growing flesh of Nazism. And that's how the camps remained for a fairly long time, until the beginning of the war. With the beginning of the war, and the invasion of Poland, the Germans found they had their hands on "the biological sources of Jewry" (those are Eichmann's words). And other concentration camps emerged, essentially different from the earlier ones. They were no longer designed to terrorize political opponents, but to destroy the Jews. These Polish camps—the three I mentioned earlier, plus some lesser ones—were "no-exit" concentration camps. They functioned without interruption, beginning in '41–'42, until the end of '43. At the end of '43—after Stalingrad—the shortage of manpower in Germany was so acute that it became indispensable to use everybody, even the Jews. It was at this time that Auschwitz emerged as a hybrid concentration camp, or rather a hybrid concentration-camp "empire": extermination plus exploitation, or rather extermination through exploitation. I owe my survival to this, namely the fact of having arrived fairly late, like all the Italian Jews, and of having been pressed into a system of production. So here was the third purpose: to have a pool of cheap, or rather no-cost, labor. This fact had been calculated in a very rational way: they anticipated a survival period of three months. There was a conflict between the political authority, the SS, which ran the camps, and German industry, which didn't care for this system, not for humanitarian reasons, but because a worker who's there for three months and then dies is a bad worker who doesn't produce. And in fact we produced very little, and this created conflicts and gave rise to protests. This dyarchy was visible to the naked eye, because at night we lived in the concentration camp, under the control of the SS, and during the day in the factory, under the authority of German industry. And these German technicians who commanded us, not that they were angels, quite the contrary, but they wanted to finish building the factory right away so as to produce rubber. And so they were opposed to a worker or prisoner getting maltreated on the job: besides, it also set a bad example, it was something *unanständig*, unseemly—go ahead and do it in the concentration camp but not here. This meant that some rather curious things happened: if someone was injured on the job, he was subject to the rules governing job accidents; it made no difference if later, once he'd returned to the concentration camp, he got sent to the gas chamber. That had nothing to do with the factory: the factory had its own rules. I remember once working in an underground metal cistern, removing the rust from the inside. It was a job like any other, no better, no worse, and the German technician had strung a light bulb by means of a wire. His superior came along and gave him a bawling out, saying, "It's very dangerous, if there should be a break in the insulation of the wire, the whole cistern would get hit by the voltage, and these men could die." So he had us all given miners' lamps. German industry was not humanitarian. But it didn't want people to die right there, for nothing. This was looked on much askance by the SS. There was even organized theft. When they needed to build a new brick barracks in the concentration camp, the SS would order us to bring four bricks each when we came back to the camp from the factory. That meant a total of forty thousand bricks, because there were ten thousand of us. They'd been stolen by the SS from industry, which kept silent, because the SS was much feared. The SS didn't care what we stole in the factory, light bulbs, axle grease, electric wiring, or whatever; and industry didn't care if we stole blankets in the camp and brought them to sell on the black market in the factory.

So, to sum up, the purposes of the concentration camp were three: terror, extermination, manpower. You also asked me, how come not a kilo of rubber was produced. That's not hard to answer. This construction site, where the factory was being built, was supposed to enter into production around the end of '43; no sooner would a notice get posted behind glass, "Production in this unit will begin on such-and-such a day," than on the day before "one" airplane would come—I don't know if it was Russian or American or what—and drop "one" bomb on the water supply or the electrical generator, paralyzing production but not destroying the factory. I think there was an agreement on this among the Allies, which meant the factory never produced anything, but it was found intact at the end of the war.

It so happened that at least thirty German readers wrote to me, all of them in response to this question: how to understand the Germans. They were all young, except for one. The first German edition came out in '61; they were young then. All of them make a point of saying that they themselves, as young Germans, don't understand themselves, much less understand their parents, because there's an insurmountable wall between them and their parents. Still others speak . . . of the devil. I've kept these letters, and now I'm going over them for a chapter in this book, *The Drowned and the Saved*. Of all those who wrote me, there was only one person who wasn't young, and he writes me a curious letter. He doesn't give his age, but you can see he's not young from what he writes. This one makes excuses for the Nazis. He's the only one. He says he wasn't a Nazi, but he declares, "We had the choice between two abysses, one was Communism, the other was Hitler; we'd seen the revolution of '19 in Germany, i.e., the Spartacist revolt, and we chose to defend ourselves; but we were betrayed. We're not a nation of traitors, we're a betrayed nation; because Hitler had promised things he didn't do and he didn't promise the things he did." This German goes on to tell me that it's not the first time massacres have occurred in the world, and maliciously mentions one I didn't know about: the massacre of the Goths carried out by the Byzantines under

Belisarius. As though to say, you Mediterraneans have also done something against us. Then he concludes: "Let's let bygones be bygones, I've fallen in love with Italy and Italian literature, and I have Dante, Petrarch, and Boccaccio in my library." It's a two-page letter. I replied that in my library I have Hitler's *Mein Kampf*, in which Hitler promised exactly what he carried out, and that he didn't betray anyone; if you can say one thing for him it's simply that he was never a deceiver. Enclosed with this man's letter was a short note from his wife, in which she says, "When the devil is loose in the village, a few people try to resist and are overcome, many bow their heads, and the majority follow him with enthusiasm." The wife had stuck this note in the envelope without her husband knowing.

Camon: Have you ever been back to Germany since the war?

Levi: Yes, I've been back at least fifteen times, on business.

Camon: Does it seem to you that there've been any profound changes?

Levi: I'd say yes, but I must tell you that my vantage point has changed, too.

Camon: If you were to give a lecture in Germany and bring up these things, do you think the

37

public would attend and be in general agreement, detached from its past?

Levi: It might have in '61; today the situation has become very complicated. Today there are symptoms of a return, if not to Nazism, at least to a right-wing, law-and-order regime, as always happens in periods of crisis. I don't actually believe there's a revival of anti-Semitism in Germany, also for a lack of raw material: there are very few Jews in Germany today.

Camon: I'm thinking of a passage in Peter Weiss's *The Investigation*, where a survivor of a concentration camp—Auschwitz, to be exact— says that every time in the summer when he boards a tram, wearing a short-sleeved shirt, and people can see the number tattooed on his arm, they look at him with an expression "of scorn."

Levi: Well . . . I don't know what to say. I must repeat that my vantage point is a peculiar one. I've been in Germany many times, alone or with my former employer, on business trips, and in short to buy things. Now it was my job to open negotiations, in my ungrammatical but anyway understandable German. They'd ask me, "How come you, being an Italian, speak German so well?" Because Italians usually don't know German. I'd tell them, "My name is Levi, you know, I'm a Jew, I was at Auschwitz." I said it openly to everyone. From that moment on the tone of the conversation changed. It became cold. Some said, "Those were bad times, my uncle died in the concentration camp, he was a politician," and so on. Whether it was true or false. But I have the feeling that for some it was true. Others said nothing, they were obviously Nazis, most of them: 99% of the Germans my age had been Nazis. Some are ashamed of it, others pretend to be ashamed, others invent a convenient past, and still others glory in it.

For the most part, our business negotiations went along in a very ordinary but correct manner. A few times I was able to talk to people "over drinks," and what usually came out were stories of fear, on their part. They'd say, "We saw terrible things, and guessed still more terrible ones." Once I was in Bavaria, to buy some raw material that's only available there in a very small factory, and there was a father-and-son pair, business partners. The father had been the local Gauleiter, and the son was a modern boy, he could just as well have been Italian or French, keen on business, without any interest whatsoever in politics. I had supper with them, and there too I had to tell my story and say I'd been at Auschwitz. The father was on pins and needles, and so was I. The son told me later that his father had been an inoffensive Gauleiter, and when the Americans came they'd shamed him in public by tying him on a tank and driving it back and forth. Nothing more. According to the son, his father's hands were clean.

Camon: It's a mystery that will pretty much remain so: what mechanism, psychologically speaking, was set off in an entire nation, and by what means.

Levi: In my opinion, the means was propaganda. It's the first case in history in which an especially powerful and violent man, a tyrant, found himself in possession of the spectacular weapon of mass communications. Mussolini, as an organizer of huge rallies, had put on a good show, but Hitler outdid him ten- or twentyfold. The Nazi ceremonies, the oaths, the rallies, had an undeniable fascination and exercised an appeal. Not for us, naturally, not for us who were "marked." When hundreds of thousands shouted "We swear!" in one voice, it was as though they'd become a single body.

Camon: So the explanation lies in that science known as mass psychology.

Levi: Yes. The manipulation of the masses was used for the first time by Fascists, Nazis, and Soviets. It couldn't have been done before: before there were no masses, there were just a few thousand people, who gathered to listen to the orator in the public square.

5. Why write?

Camon: Somewhere you've said that your purpose in writing was "for inner liberation." But let's analyze this statement a little more closely. Why have you written? In order to denounce? Thereby to demand justice? To arrive at an understanding of an enigma, a mystery, "the mystery of Germany," the "madness of Germany"? Writing as an appeal to others for help in the solution? Writing as consolation? Out of all this, what was that "inner liberation" you were trying to achieve through writing supposed to be?

Levi: Your question has to do only with *Survival in Auschwitz*. I wrote because I felt the need to write. If you ask me to go further and find out what produced this need, I can't answer. I've had the feeling that for me the act of writing was equivalent to lying down on Freud's couch. I felt such an overpowering need to talk about it that I talked out loud. Back then, in the concentration camp, I often had a dream: I dreamed that I'd returned, come home to my family, told them about it, and nobody listened. The person standing in front of me doesn't stay to hear, he turns around and goes away. I told this dream to my friends in the concentration camp, and they said, "It happens to us too."

And later I found it mentioned, in the very same way, by other survivors who've written about their experiences. So we're dealing with a typical situation.

Camon: So was it your collective unconscious that felt that experience to be incredible, at the very moment you were all living it?

Levi: Yes. But this dream of talking about it was certainly comparable to the dream of Tantalus, which was of "eating—almost," of being able to bring the food to one's mouth but not succeeding in biting into it. It's the dream of a primary need, the need to eat and drink. So was the need to talk about it. Already at the time it was a basic need. Later I chose to write it as the equivalent of talking about it.

Camon: Talking about it more extensively, in time and space, to more people and over a longer period of time, to be believed finally by everyone, since in the dream even your family didn't believe you?

Levi: Yes. The nightmare of the dream, however, was still inside me. While I was writing *Survival in Auschwitz*, I wasn't sure it would be published. I wanted to make four or five copies, and give them to my fiancée and friends. My writing was therefore a way of telling them about it. The intention to "leave an eyewitness account" came later, the primary need was to write for purposes of liberation.

Camon: To write, that is, for therapeutic purposes.

Levi: Yes, therapeutic.

Camon: And in that sense did it work?

Levi: Yes, writing relieved me.

6. Nazi camps and Communist camps

Camon: I recall now that we've exchanged letters about this concentration-camp theme—to be exact, about the comparison between Nazi and Communist camps. Because the concentration camp also represents the "impulse to write" for another, very different, contemporary writer: Solzhenitsyn. But we're dealing with two different kinds of concentration camp, and two different literary operations, which, in my opinion (as I've written in my book *Avanti popolo*), cannot be compared. I'll sum up my own thoughts, which I'd like, if I may, to examine alongside yours: Solzhenitsyn is the spokesman for those who have paid with their lives for the "deviations" of socialism, while you're the spokesman for those who have paid for the "consistency" of Nazism. What I mean is that in Ivan Denisovich's concentration camp there's a voice of protest among the prisoners and against the authorities (and which sometimes even gets uttered) that runs like this: "You're not Soviets! You're not Communists!" But in Primo Levi's concentration camp, the accusation is not that of breaking faith with an idea, but of fully carrying it out, which means it's an accusation that goes like this: "You're perfect Nazis, you're the embodiment of your idea."

Levi: I agree completely. It seems to me a perfect distinction.

Camon: So, in reading *One Day in the Life of Ivan Denisovich*, you don't feel any identification? And what do you feel in reading *Ivan Denisovich*?

Levi: I read *Ivan Denisovich* with a red and blue pencil in my hand, marking in red the things that had been the same for us, and in blue the things that were different. Well, there are many things in common. In the first place, the lack of solidarity. There the prisoner is called a *zek*. And who is the *zek*'s worst enemy? Another *zek*—and this completely corresponds to my own experience. Then, Ivan Denisovich has been selected by Solzhenitsyn as one who's already been through the mill, he's the equivalent of what among us was called "a low number," someone who now knows how to *organisieren*, which means to operate illegally. The word has roughly the same meaning all over Europe: *organizzare, organiser, organisieren*. The *zek* Ivan Denisovich is an operator. But our disagreement about *One Day in the Life of Ivan Denisovich* hinged on something else.

Camon: We'll get to that in a moment. In Ivan Denisovich the experience seems to be less horrible, his concentration camp seems to me less demoniacal.

Levi: That stems from the fact that there are Russians both inside and outside: the *zek* is not an alien. The racial factor is lacking and so is the linguistic one.

Camon: You felt the language barrier very much, I see.

Levi: Very much. Because I'm a talker. If you stop up my mouth, I die. And there they stopped up my mouth.

Camon: And the others, how did they feel it?

Levi: The others died. Even if they didn't realize that that was why they were dying.

Camon: So not being able to communicate by speech was fatal?

Levi: It was physically fatal. They had the feeling they were dying of cold or hunger, and there was that too, of course, but the primary cause was the linguistic isolation. If you look at the statis-

47

tics, the Jews of Central Europe, Jews who spoke German, survived in at least ten times greater proportion than we did. I remember a Croatian Jew who, as soon as he got there, yelled out, "I speak German, I can be an interpreter for you." And he became an interpreter. I myself must say that the little German I knew was precious to me, and that, fairly consciously, I forced myself in the concentration camp to absorb German from the air around me. As a result my survivor's German was the German of the SS and the Wehrmacht, and I didn't realize it. I said things that I shouldn't have said, rather like someone who's learned Italian in a whorehouse.

Camon: Our disagreement about Solzhenitsyn came from the fact that I don't consider him a great writer.

Levi: But he's saved by *Ivan Denisovich*, that one book anyway, and also by parts of *The First Circle*. In *Ivan Denisovich* I found all the material details told extremely well: how you eat your soup, how you manage to get by, how you dress, how you hide things if there's a search, how you work—even that curious item about the pride you feel at having built a straight wall. Under such conditions, work can be salvation, if you're able to perceive that the work is useful. I remember one of my fellow workers (the one who didn't want to steal, remember?), he wanted us to do a good job so as to be able to feel some gratification at the end of the day. I can understand that. Even the Germans, however, had understood it, although in previous experiments they made people do grossly useless tasks, like shoveling dirt from here to there and then back again, or digging trenches and then filling them up. As I said before, when they began to feel the scarcity of manpower they gave up this tormenting use of labor. Work was still very hard, but not pointless.

But getting back to Solzhenitsyn, I find that he's very good at describing conditions in the concentration camp. From that standpoint there's nothing to fault him for.

Camon: I've also faulted him for seeing the history of Communism as an exact continuation of czarism. For not having noted any break, and in short for having a "Western" and "capitalist" view of Russian history.

Levi: That's true. He even bemoans czarism; in *The Gulag Archipelago* he says so clearly.

Camon: We were talking about the concentration camp. And therefore Germany. What does Germany mean to you today? Are you able to separate your opinion of Germany and the German people from your experience of the concentration camp? Do you think, as Brecht said, that "the womb / that gave birth to the foul thing / is still fruitful"?

49

Levi: It may be that I am indulging in "wishful thinking,"[1] that I have such repugnance for Nazi Germany that I can't even tolerate the idea that it might rise again. Birth from such a womb is intolerable to me, and so I try to convince myself that the womb is no longer fruitful. Maybe it is. But, on the other hand, I've been to Germany, and I know how many Germans take their vacations in Italy, France, Yugoslavia, and Spain. A phenomenon like that, of total cultural isolation, is no longer conceivable. And I believe that Nazism, and what came afterwards, including Germany's division in two, works like a vaccination, at least for a few decades.

Camon: A literary question: today *Survival in Auschwitz* is an exemplary text in what is called "concentration-camp literature." It's a classic. But how was it possible for the manuscript, having been submitted for publication, to have been rejected for so many years? In other words, I mean here's a book that today seems to us necessary and indispensable (as every classic is); didn't the right conditions exist as soon as the war was over for it to be understood and accepted?

Levi: It's true that it took several years before the manuscript was accepted, and what's always surprised me is that the person who'd read it is an important figure in Italian literature, Jewish,

---

1. In English in the original.

and still alive. If you turn off the tape recorder, I'll tell you who it is. [*I turn it off and he tells me.*] The reasons were very vague—they were the usual ones that publishers give when they send back a manuscript. I don't know why it was rejected. Maybe it was just the fault of an inattentive reader.

7. *The birth of Israel*

Camon: I've thought from time to time that the history of the Jews is one thing up until the founding of Israel, and afterwards something else. Because at first the Jews were a stateless people reaching out toward a state. Thus they had a pole of convergence in their future, their history moved in a centripetal direction. But the state of Israel, for reasons of security, soon began to act on its surroundings with an expansionist drive, thus in a centrifugal direction. And from that moment on the history of the Jews has profoundly changed, sometimes to the point of taking on an aggressive and destructive role.

Levi: Yes, yes, of course. But only insofar as the history of the "state" is concerned. Here's what the state of Israel was intended for, and it was supposed to change the history of the Jewish people, but in a very precise sense: it was supposed to be a life raft, the sanctuary to which Jews threatened in other countries would be able to run. That was the idea of the founding fathers, and it preceded the Nazi tragedy: the Nazi tragedy multiplied it a thousandfold. Jews could no longer do without that country of salvation. Nobody stopped to think that there were Arabs in that country. In truth there weren't very many. And it was considered a negligible fact compared with this tremendous driving force that was sending Jews there from all over Europe.

Camon: If my memory doesn't deceive me, during the first Arab-Israeli war there were a few European (German) intellectuals who left to fight on Israel's side, almost as a concrete demonstration of the wave of solidarity with Israel. Perhaps in this way they also wanted to expiate the historical sin of their fathers. But they could also proclaim (I'm quoting from memory) that "no state was as legitimate and moral as the state of Israel." Today—after Israel's most recent war, the invasion of Lebanon along with the episodes of refugee camps being annihilated—I think that such a gesture, such a statement, would sound impossible and even culpable. I mention these episodes as confirmation of my thesis that the history of the Jews has indeed split into two phases: before and after Israel.

Levi: In my opinion, Israel is taking on the nature and behavior of its neighbors. I say it with sorrow and anger. There's not much difference among Begin, Arafat, and Khomeini. They are people who don't respect agreements. But Begin represented a country that's at least nominally democratic . . .

Camon: It's very united, Israel . . .

Levi: No, not any more. The army is disciplined, but the country is no longer unified.

Camon: But a prime minister who commits such acts in any other country would have fallen.

Levi: Yes, Begin kept a majority. But initially it was a substantial majority, then not any more. I'm well aware that those who voted for him were the new immigrants, immigrants from Arab countries, uprooted young refugees from Egypt, Syria, and Libya. They'd been deprived of their property and kicked out. It's understandable that they saw their leader in Begin, who was anti-Arab. There's a very sharp gap between this Israeli element, which is now the majority, and the old immigrants and their children, who had a European background. Begin was an old terrorist, already from the time he was in Poland.

Camon: That's an accusation that many Jews of the Diaspora reject.

Levi: Yes, I know. But there are different ways of being a Jew. Every Jew has the right and duty to choose his position: religious or non-religious, pro-Israel or anti-Israel. I must admit to feeling a sentimental tie with Israel, if for no other reason than it was built by us, by my fellow prisoners. But I don't recognize myself at all in its present behavior, in not keeping its word. Begin had said he'd go forty kilometers, and he went all the way to Beirut. On the other hand, it's obvious that there's an element of necessity in all this, until the PLO charter gets changed. And Begin didn't want it to change, because it's been his alibi.

Camon: So if there are "two phases" in Jewish history, *If Not Now, When?* is the saga of the first phase, the story of a people "on its way toward." In short, you constitute the tragic preamble (*Survival in Auschwitz, The Reawakening*) of the first phase, and the story of the passage (*If Not Now, When?*) from the first phase to the second. But the new history of the Jews evades these preambles and prophecies.

Levi: Some things haven't changed and don't change: for instance, the situation of Jews in the Soviet Union. It's a terrible situation, not like that of the Jews in Germany, but like the one under Stalin. The Jews are subjected to awful and changeable pressure. One hundred or five hundred emigration visas are granted each month, depending on whether international tension is rising or falling. Israel still represents a goal for all Russian Jews.

8. *The works*

Camon: Your literary works and those on scientific subjects (*Storie naturali, Vizio di forma*) are so different from the works on the "concentration-camp condition" as to raise a question about their author: what's surprising is that these "divertissements" (as you've called *Storie naturali*) are written by the same author as the books on the concentration camp. But I'd go even further and say that since *Storie naturali* was written simultaneously with *The Reawakening*, it would therefore indicate a kind of split in their author, a dual operation of his mind.

This is shown, in my opinion, by the different name used by the author: Damiano Malabaila. It may be that the pseudonym was suggested by fear and modesty, but at a deeper level it may well have been suggested by his awareness of being not one author but two—of being, so to speak, divided.

Levi: That's a question that you can answer better than I. I mean I can't answer. I don't even know of any test or mental experiment that one could do to verify it.

Before they arrested me I'd already written a short story, of which I still have a copy, but I've been careful not to publish it. It was a mediocre arabesque, with a little of everything in it.

Camon: Maybe without the experience of the concentration camp, you would have been a writer all the same (I'm convinced of it—there's no way you wouldn't have been a writer), but an ironical, fantastic, allegorical, esoteric, scientific, naturalist writer.

Levi: Actually in that first story there's a lot of the natural world, rocks and plants. Yes, perhaps that's what I would have written about; I was fascinated by that world. But for me the experience of the concentration camp has been fundamental. Naturally I wouldn't do it all over again, but still, along with the horror of that experience, which I still feel now, I can't deny that it's also had positive results. It seems to me that that was where I learned to know the facts about people. There's a friend of mine, Lidia Roffi, who was in Ravensbrück, she was a schoolteacher, and she says that Ravensbrück was her university. It was the only concentration camp strictly for women. I'd been to the university, but I too must say that my real university was Auschwitz. I have the feeling of having been enriched by it, so much so that it took me only a few months to write *Survival in Auschwitz*, and I remember writing it without ever faltering. When it was published by Einaudi in 1958, I inserted one chapter, the one about initiation, which isn't in the De Silva edition of 1947, and I added quite a lot, but I didn't change, delete, or correct anything.

Camon: There are sufferings that make us better people and sufferings that make us worse. Probably those experienced in a state of powerlessness make us better.

Levi: I don't think I became a better person. I understood a few things, but that didn't make me good.

Camon: How many prisoners were there, on the average, every day in Auschwitz?

Levi: There wasn't just one Auschwitz camp; there were thirty-nine of them. There was the town of Auschwitz, and in it was a concentration camp, and that was Auschwitz properly speaking, or the capital of the system. Down below, two kilometers away, was Birkenau, or

Auschwitz Two: here they had the gas chamber; it was a huge concentration camp, divided into some four to six adjoining camps. Farther up was the factory, and near the factory was Monowitz, or Auschwitz Three: that's where I was. This camp belonged to the factory, it had been financed by it. In addition, all around, there were thirty to thirty-five small camps (mines, arms factories, farms, etc.). The most distant camp was Brno, in Moravia: it was about a hundred kilometers away, as the crow flies, and was under the administration of Auschwitz. In my camp there were about ten thousand of us; in central Auschwitz fifteen or twenty thousand; in Birkenau many more, seventy to eighty thousand; plus another twenty thousand scattered about in these little camps, which were all frightful places, mines, where you worked amid cold and hunger; they were punishment camps. But Auschwitz One was the administrative center for all of them, and Birkenau was the extermination camp. The Auschwitz system was the fruit of experience gathered in all the other camps, both for extermination and forced labor. There's a book about it, in fact the diary of the Auschwitz commandant, who when he was captured was asked to tell his story, and he did.[1]

---

1. Rudolf Höss, *Commandant of Auschwitz*, London, 1959.

Camon: You're not a depressed man, and not even anxious.

Levi: Is that a feeling you get from my books or from my presence?

Camon: From your presence. You have an ironical and tolerant attitude, and you often smile. I have the feeling that by nature you're someone who loves life, who loved it before, and who loves it afterwards. Between the before and the after there's been a violent and total trauma, but it's over.

Levi: In general, you're right. Since the concentration camp, however, I've had a few attacks of depression. I'm not sure if they go back to that experience, because they come with different labels, from one to the next. It may seem strange to you, but I went through one just recently, a stupid fit of depression, for very little reason: I had a small operation on my foot, and this made me think that I'd suddenly got old. It took two months for the wound to heal. That's why I asked you if the feeling came from my presence or my books.

Camon: I said from your presence, but it's not that your books contradict it. In your scientific and naturalist works one is aware of a fantastic, allegorical writer, with a language full of life, and a display of metaphor.

Levi: While I wasn't at all interested in the problem of language when I wrote *Survival in Auschwitz*, it gradually began to interest me the more I went on writing, until it became uppermost in *The Monkey's Wrench*, which is an experimental book. And also in this recent book, *If Not Now, When?*, in which I've been faced with linguistic problems, because it was a matter of having people speak in Italian—of translating into Italian—dialogue that was supposed to be in Polish or Russian or Yiddish. I don't know either Polish or Russian, and my Yiddish is poor, and so I had to study up on on it, which I did. I studied Yiddish for eight months, so as to be able to give to these characters an Italian speech that would sound plausible as a translation. I don't know if the average Italian reader is aware of these things.

Camon: After the first books, the ones on the concentration camp, one feels this interest in words, in language, and even a taste for experiment. That's why it seems strange to me that you didn't become a literary writer, but went on applying yourself to chemistry and being a chemist.

Levi: But I was always interested in chemistry, and in school I was lazy and bored, and poor in Italian. As a student I didn't understand the importance of Italian literature; I understood it later.

9. Chemistry and the man

Camon: But what is it in chemistry that interests you?

Levi: I'm interested in the contact with matter, in understanding the world around me; I'm interested in the chemistry of the human body, biochemistry. In short, science: but the science of particles doesn't say much to me, while I'm thrilled by the discovery of genetic mechanisms, the way the individual is coded, the minuscule chain whose alphabet is made up of molecules. There's a bridge between linguists and geneticists. These new concepts of "pregnancy," of "redundance," of "ambiguity," apply very well to the language of genetics, and genetic failures are due to the lack of redundancy, for which it takes only the slightest error and the reading is broken. But the reasons that brought me to chemistry were different at that time, because chemistry was then a different science. I chose to get interested in chemistry when I was a boy—I was fourteen or fifteen—because I was thrilled by the parallel between the formula written on paper and what takes place in the test tube. Already then it seemed to me something magical, and chemistry seemed to me the main key to open the secrets of heaven and earth, and having read at the time that a spectroscope allows you to know the chemical composition of a star, it seemed to me one of man's greatest powers.

Camon: So, chemistry and literature; concentration-camp writer, and scientific and naturalist writer. The fact that the literary writing came after the concentration-camp books suggests that the Auschwitz trauma had receded almost to the point of disappearing and that it wasn't simply negative. How about at the private, personal, family level?

Levi: No, as I said, Auschwitz was not simply negative for me, it taught me a lot. Among other things, before Auschwitz I was a man with no woman, afterwards I met the one who was to become my wife. I very much needed someone to listen to me, and she listened more than others. That's why, in sickness and in health, I'm bound to her for life. Before that I was full of complexes, I don't know why. Maybe because I was a Jew. As a Jew, I'd been made fun of by my schoolmates: not beaten up, or insulted, but made fun of, yes.

After my return from Auschwitz, I had a great need to talk, I looked up my old friends and talked their ears off, and I remember their saying to me, "How strange! You haven't changed a bit." I think I'd undergone a process of maturing, having had the luck to survive. Because it's not a question of strength, but of luck: you can't beat a concentration camp with your own strengths. I'd been lucky: for having been a chemist, for having met a bricklayer who gave me something to eat, for having overcome the language difficulty (this I can claim to have done); I never got sick—I got sick only once, at the end, and this too was lucky, because I missed the evacuation of the camp. The others, the healthy ones, all died because they were transferred to Buchenwald and Mauthausen in the middle of winter. I had an argument . . . are you a believer?

Camon: Why do you ask?

Levi: I had an argument with a believer, a friend of mine from Padua, your city, by the way.

Camon: You're not a believer?

Levi: No, I never have been. I'd like to be, but I don't succeed.

Camon: Then in what sense are you Jewish?

Levi: A simple matter of culture. If it hadn't been for the racial laws and the concentration camp, I'd probably no longer be a Jew, except for my last name. Instead, this dual experience, the racial laws and the concentration camp, stamped me the way you stamp a steel plate. At this point I'm a Jew, they've sewn the star of David on me and not only on my clothes.

Camon: With whom did you have that argument?

Levi: If you remember *The Periodic Table*, he's the one mentioned as "the assistant" in the "Potassium" story. He's a believer but not a Catholic; he came to see me after my release to tell me I was clearly one of the elect, since I'd been chosen to survive in order for me to write *Survival in Auschwitz*. And this, I must confess, seemed to me a blasphemy, that God should grant privileges, saving one person and condemning someone else. I must say that for me the experience of Auschwitz has been such as to sweep away any remnant of religious education I may have had.

Camon: Meaning that Auschwitz is proof of the nonexistence of God?

Levi: There is Auschwitz, and so there cannot be God. [*On the typescript, he added in pencil*: I don't find a solution to this dilemma. I keep looking, but I don't find it.]

even his fellow prisoners (and they included scientists, clergymen, musicians, politicians) had not understood or fixed in their memory, and he was able to do so because *he was a writer.* In the chemical laboratory, in the barracks, at roll call, during the selection of prisoners for the gas chamber, in his encounters with other inmates and with the SS, the gaze, memory, and silence of Primo Levi were the gaze, memory, and silence of a writer.

In 1832 the Italian patriot Silvio Pellico published *Le mie prigioni*, an account of his years of confinement in Austrian prisons, at the time when Austria ruled northern Italy. This book is said to have been "more damaging to Austria than a lost battle." Much more could be said of Primo Levi's first book, *Survival in Auschwitz*, his memories of the concentration camp: it has been more damaging to Germany than the lost war. The war was a military defeat, albeit of such proportions as to uproot and overturn the order of Europe and the world, but the book testifies to a moral defeat from which the German conscience has not yet recovered. In recent years there has been a good deal of debate in Europe on a question that has broken out in Germany among historians; it concerns the Nazi past, which in Germany they call "a past that hasn't passed." German society is at a loss to know what can be done to redeem that guilt, how to be reconciled with the fact of "being born

German." And it speaks enviously of the younger generation of Germans, those who have had the "good fortune to be born late." The philosopher Habermas has invented a novel theory, one that allows the concept of "nationality" to be reinvented: it would no longer consist in a hereditary "given" (one is already a German by virtue of being born), but would include a certain degree of reinvention, and hence of will. Each generation would reconstruct the manner in which it belongs to the nation, rethink its relationship with its forefathers, choose its own forefathers, and modify and correct them. A marvelous idea, in a university lecture hall: it no doubt gets a round of applause from the students. It ought to be engraved on the tombstone of the man who uttered it. But something quite different is needed to reconcile a people with its history. The writer Günter Grass confesses that, as an heir to that history, he still today feels a "growing shame." The truth is that the problem of "absolute evil" (mass extermination) remains a mystery: not only has a solution (assuming there is one) not been found, but the problem has not even been properly stated. We still do not know, not only "why" it happened, but "how" it happened, i.e., what the facts are. For those who have told us "how" have been very few. One of them is Primo Levi.

Primo Levi's testimony is not testimony to "evil" at its highest degree. At its highest degree,

71

"evil" cannot be testified to, cannot be described. The witnesses who have seen it at this degree do not speak, nor will they ever speak. When Claude Lanzmann, the French film director and editor of the magazine *Les Temps Modernes* (founded and directed by Sartre), set out to interview the survivors of the concentration camps, he encountered the greatest reluctance and incapacity on their part to speak. His film *Shoah* is imbued with an anguish that goes beyond words. The witnesses weep before the camera, they tremble, and seem anxious to escape, and when they do speak, their words are inadequate to describe what they ought to be describing. Levi is thus not a witness to "evil" at this level: he would not have written. But he is a witness at the highest level at which "evil" can be described. Beyond that limit, even Levi would be struck dumb.

Levi was sent to the concentration camp late, a year before the arrival of the Red Army. As a chemist, his situation there was a privileged one. He gained possession of a fundamental tool for survival: an understanding of the German language. A further and fundamental detail: he did not get sick when sickness would have cost him his life (i.e., when gas-chamber victims were selected), and he did get sick when health would have cost him his life (i.e., when the camp was evacuated). A series of coincidences allowed him to pass through Hell and come out on the other side. And live to tell about it.

Levi's testimony was so new and traumatic that in the beginning no one even listened. Indeed, his first book was read in manuscript and rejected by the editors at Einaudi, then the most prestigious publisher in Italy. To make matters worse, the manuscript was read by a Jewish writer, Natalia Ginzburg (the name can be surmised for the first time from these *Conversations with Primo Levi*). To this day Ginzburg is unable to justify her rejection, for which there can be only one explanation: either from immaturity or insensitivity, she had not understood the book. But Levi's works continued to meet this fate even after publication, when the problem arose of their being translated abroad. The German language received them late and with controversy (which now, with the translation of *The Drowned and the Saved*, is being revived), and the French never entirely accepted them, at least while Levi was alive. I still remember how I kept urging Gallimard, my French publisher, to translate *The Drowned and the Saved*, but to no avail: they always replied that the book would have no success. How wrong they were! Today we can say that in France too (Gallimard having finally been convinced) Levi has become a "classic," a writer we cannot do without, a writer for everyone and for all time.

73

Levi had an inkling of this destiny: in a letter I received a couple of days after his death, and which was written a couple of days before it, he expressed a number of hopes and expectations (especially for the French translation), and told me his wishes and plans for the future. It is not a letter by someone thinking of suicide, but rather by someone who hasn't the slightest intention of ceasing to live and struggle. This is why his death (he fell down the stairwell of the building where he lived) seems to me an accident, not a voluntary act. People in Italy are inclined to say that he killed himself because he had finished his work, concluded (with *The Drowned and the Saved*) his testimony. But that was not the way it was: shortly before his death he was still listing the things that had to be done, because his testimony had not yet arrived in those parts of the world where it was needed the most. And who knows if it will ever arrive.

How is it that, on first impact, Levi so often turns out to be unacceptable? The fact is that his very strength, the enormity of the things to which he bears witness, constitute his handicap. Europe's conscience is crushed by it, and would like to be able to free itself. But it is society's task to prevent this. Levi's works are widely read in Italian schools, and it would be a good thing if they were also to make an appearance in German schools and those in the Soviet Union, Iran, the Middle East, and elsewhere. Not many people know that the Soviet Union has always refused to allow the publication of Levi's books in Russian, because of the parallel one can feel in Levi between Hitler's Nazi concentration camps and Stalin's Communist ones. Only in the last few years has this refusal been somewhat attenuated. The camp where Levi was, Auschwitz, in Poland, was liberated by the Red Army. Levi's testimony ends with some Russian soldiers, who without speaking gaze—mute with horror—at the interior of the camp. No, not with horror, but with shame. And here is something that it is difficult to understand, but which *must* be understood. There was Auschwitz, and humanity was ashamed of itself. All of humanity, including those who had no part in it, and knew nothing about it. Since then this "shame" of humanity has never let up. Levi arouses shame, and this is the obstacle to his widespread acceptance. As soon as they saw him at Auschwitz, his liberators felt an intolerable embarrassment. Since then, every other Soviet citizen has been shielded from that shame. And yet this liberation can never be said to have been brought to a conclusion so long as a writer thus liberated is not allowed to tell his story to his liberators.

Levi lived in Turin, in northwest Italy. Turin is the Detroit of Europe: it contains the largest automobile factory on the Old Continent. It is a mysterious city for the rest of Italy: Italy knows Milan, Rome, and Naples much better—Turin is

75

CONTEMPORARY AND MODERN
ITALIAN WRITING
FROM THE MARLBORO PRESS

MARIO BRELICH:

The Work of Betrayal. Translated by Raymond Rosenthal. 1989.

FERDINANDO CAMON:

The Fifth Estate. Translated by John Shepley. 1987.

Life Everlasting. Translated by John Shepley. 1988.

Memorial. Translated by David Calicchio. 1983.

The Story of Sirio. Translated by Cassandra Bertea. 1985.

GABRIELE D'ANNUNZIO:

Nocturne and Five Tales of Love and Death. Translated by Raymond Rosenthal. 1988.

CURZIO MALAPARTE:

Kaputt. Translated by Cesare Foligno. 1982.

The Skin. Translated by David Moore. 1988.

MARIA MESSINA:

A House in the Shadows. Translated by John Shepley. 1989.

PIER PAOLO PASOLINI:

Roman Nights and Other Stories. Translated by John Shepley. 1986.

ALBERTO SAVINIO:

> *Capri.* Translated by John Shepley. 1989.

> *Operatic Lives.* Translated by John Shepley. 1988.

> *Speaking to Clio.* Translated by John Shepley. 1987.

ELIO VITTORINI:

> *Men and Not Men.* Translated by Sarah Henry. 1985.

ᴛ**M**ᴾ

2812-10
5-09
C